A Trilogy of Healing

A Trilogy of Healing

Poetry for the Broken Hearted

GLENN GOREE

Foreword by Don Lambert

RESOURCE *Publications* · Eugene, Oregon

Resource Publications
An Imprint of Wipf and Stock Publishers
199 W. 8th Ave., Suite 3
Eugene, OR 97401

www.wipfandstock.com

PAPERBACK ISBN: 978–1-5326–6855–5
HARDCOVER ISBN: 978–1-5326–6856–2
EBOOK ISBN: 978–1-5326–6857–9

Manufactured in the U.S.A.   NOVEMBER 7, 2018

I dedicate this work to the most important woman in my life, my wife Valerie, my anchor and light.

Contents

Foreword

As a young man growing up in what was then Rhodesia, I had always heard story's about Texas and how big everything was in Texas" . . . .When I met Glenn after his arrival in my hometown of Bulawayo, I started to believe the stories . . . Tall, broad of shoulder, thighs like tree trunks and arms like steam engine pistons . . . Glenn stood out as the quintessentaial example of the what someone from Texas would look like, if you held those stories to be true . . . Apart from his physical stature I also learnt some other things about this man from Texas . . . His love, compassion, generosity and kindness were likewise Texas sized . . . He became and to this day is still someone whose presence I actively seek when I have the chance to travel anywhere near the place he and his wife reside . . .

When you read these poems you will start to know a lot more about him than I can ascribe to him in a few sentences . . .

Deeply convicted of his beliefs through a journey of life that moulded him into a man of God who knows the pain of separation and then redemption that God has offered to all those who seek His path . . . These poems truly encapsulate the wonder that is our Creator and our God . . . They are insightful, passionate, heartfelt and inspirational and would be worthy additions to anyone seeking comfort in the promises, made and kept, of Gods Forgiveness, Mercy and Grace . . . .

Glenn has one more Texas sized attribute that I believe is revealed by this Anthology in Poems of Gods wonderful plan for us . . . His heart . . .

Texas sized for sure, but Heavenward bound . . . Glenn is a man I am honoured to call friend, confidant, brother in Christ, of whom I can offer no greater compliment but to quote my favourite verse in support of these outstanding poems . . .

> 38 For I am persuaded, that neither death, nor life, nor angels, nor principalities, nor powers, nor things present, nor things to come,

39 Nor height, nor depth, nor any other creature, shall be able to separate us from the love of God, which is in Christ Jesus our Lord.

ROMANS 8:38–39 KJV

DON LAMBERT
2018

Anthology One

A WORLD WITHOUT FORGIVENESS

"The Lord is compassionate and gracious; slow to anger, abounding in love. He will not always accuse, nor will he harbor his anger forever; he does not treat us as our sins deserve or repay us according to our iniquities. For as high as the heavens are above the earth, so great is his love for those who fear him; as far as the east is from the west, so far has he removed our transgressions from us. As a father has compassion on his children, so the Lord has compassion on those who fear him; for he knows how we are formed, he remembers that we are dust."

(PSALM 103:8–14) NIV

Forgiveness Unprecedented

IMAGINE A WORLD WITHOUT forgiveness. There would be wars, famine, hunger, pestilence, murder, rape, and many other perils. Oh, wait a minute, we have those problems now and forgiveness has been a part of our world since its beginning. Now think what our world would be like if the divine blessing of forgiveness didn't exist at all.

Forgiveness is a difficult virtue to practice much less fulfill when feelings have been bruised. And yet, when forgiveness is offered and accepted it is the most powerful medicine for the soul. Friendships are reborn, marriages are healed, co-workers grow more in tandem in their relationships, and small children learn to play well together by sharing their sandbox equally and fairly.

You may think the idea of two children learning to play nicely together in a sandbox is inconsequential to forgiveness. But practicing this virtue, or refusing to, forms the core of the adult heart. The only difference between the lesson on forgiveness a child and an adult can either learn or fail to learn is found in the size of their sandbox. Are not corporate wars fought over the size of respective company sandboxes? And how about military wars? Were not The Great War and World War II fought over the size of sandboxes? In both the corporate wars and world wars, the opponents were/are jealous not only of the size of the sandboxes but what was/is in them as well. And usually adults who can't play nicely with each other didn't play well in a sandbox as a child either.

What, then, do I mean when I say *forgiveness unauthorized*? Other than to catch a reader's attention, this snappy title and the titles of the following poems have a deeper, spiritual single-mindedness.

God's forgiveness is intended for all people everywhere. What if Jesus had said while hanging on the cross, "Father because these people are murdering me I don't want them to be forgiven."

No, his words were, "Father forgive them for they know not what they do." (Luke 23:34)

Jesus chose to forgive his foes even though they were in the very act of murdering him. They had witnessed the Roman soldiers fillet his back with whips until his flesh had been torn from his body exposing his ribs. They didn't cringe as iron nails were driven into his hands and feet. And in a final insult to injury, they stood at the foot of his cross and watched his life blood pour down his body.

So how could Jesus pray to his Father to grant these hypocrites forgiveness? Was not their goal to murder Jesus? Jesus asked for them to be forgiven even though he knew they chose not to understand. Understand what? They chose not to understand the bigger picture. They weren't murdering a mere man; they were murdering the Son of God.

Their focus of concern was on this life and not the next. They chose not to acknowledge he was the Son of God by turning a blind eye to his miracles and a deaf ear to his teachings. And yet, regardless of their lack of spiritual acuity he still did not want to punish them.

With Christ's example on the cross, how can any of us refuse to receive or offer forgiveness? Not one human has suffered the gravity of Christ's injustice. Through his example, we should be inspired to offer and receive forgiveness no matter what the circumstance. Is this practice of humility difficult? Do any of us think it was easy for Jesus to ask God to forgive the people who were murdering him? No, it wasn't easy because although his divine mission was to die, his human side dreaded making the ultimate sacrifice. In the end, his divinity took precedence over his humanity, an act for which we should be eternally grateful.

Hence, what does this background to Christ's forgiveness have to do with the title of the first section of poems? Christians live in a secular world that does not believe in forgiveness. It believes in payback, or in saying, "I forgive", but the words are empty, a ruse. Some people embrace forgiveness for a time, but later stab the forgiven in the back. The world takes a variety of false actions that avoid the true meaning of forgiveness.

This spiritual disrespect for forgiveness can only lead to the conclusion that forgiveness in the secular world is not authorized, and—sad to say—sometimes in the Christian world as well. Extend a hand in forgiveness but don't mean it. Agree in love but live in resentment. Hold a grudge, develop bitterness, become cynical, and be acerbic.

I believe the most damaging relationship where people will not authorize forgiveness is in their connection with God. Cognitively, they know God has forgiven them, but emotionally they will not acknowledge his forgiveness. They feel they have committed one sin too many, or perhaps committed the unpardonable sin. Either way, they believe their sinful behavior will not pass God's eternal muster. These poems address this self-condemning rationale. You will discover a theme that not only authorizes God's forgiveness but embraces you in his light. These poems communicate a message that's not theological but Biblical. They aren't about the logic of forgiveness, but center on the joy and relief God's forgiveness brings to the restored person's life

> Anger harbored is resentment moored.
> Forgiveness extended is grace shored.
> Mercy received is love restored.

A WORLD WITHOUT FORGIVENESS

Please ponder a moment or two,
Focus your mind on what you could do.

If we lived in a world without forgiveness,
Can you imagine the irrational stress?

Then imagine if you will,
How our hearts would grow cold and still,

In a world devoid of trust and love,
Not from man to man, nor from above.

For God has shown us the example supreme,
To teach us how not to be vile and mean.

By giving us his son on the cross,
He counts death a victory, not a loss.

He demonstrated a model unique,
Which each of us should always seek,

To lay aside our anger from sins of another,
And call one and all to be our brother.

FORGIVENESS PATRONIZED

"What is truth?" Pilate asked,
Seeking favor in which to bask.

The crowd chose death over forgiveness; he washed his hands,
When in truth a pardon he could command.

"Stone her! Stone her!" The teachers of the Mosaic Law demanded.
Was there concern for the adulteress or how their reputation with the
crowd would stand?

Forgiveness was staring these mobs in their veiled eyes,
It was the five-hundred-pound camel amid patronizing lies.

Perhaps this is one reason Jesus is so attractive to the hurting soul,
You get what you see and hear—no deceit in part or in whole.

Forgiveness is real and genuine, one hundred percent;
Jesus offers full pardon, sent from heaven, express.

FORGIVENESS HYPOTHESIZED

What if I said, "I'm sorry."?
Could these two words alone create a new romantic story?

For couples torn asunder by passion's storming thunder,
Because of pride's blunder causing a marriage to sink under.

OK. Here's another olive branch for those willing to take humility's
chance.
"I was wrong and you were right. Please, I don't want to fight."

Soothing words to the ear and soul,
Turning anger's flame into a cool, white coal,

Perhaps now I'm becoming too personal,
Daring to challenge our self-first arsenal.

Oh, but with forgiveness's sweet surrender,
There return moments exquisite and tender,

Could this hypothesis of forgiveness be a reality
That was first granted from the garden's fruit tree?

And is this hope not what Jesus had in mind,
When his flesh and blood with the cross became entwined?

Because he has a love, unique and rare,
Let us embrace that which Satan dares.

Our Father in heaven has much in store—
Forgiveness is the key that unlocks the door.

FORGIVENESS CHARACTERIZED

Forgiveness characterized,
Seems an unusual phrase not just for my eyes.

But what, pray tell,
Will sound an alarm in character's bell,

That presents a wholesome depiction,
Not based in science fiction,

Of a soul once dark but now seeks the light,
And is prepared to defend its newfound honor in a holy fight?

And in place of bitter brine,
Now drinks our Savior's wine.

But doesn't stop there,
Because it seeks with gentle care,

To feast on his flesh,
So he's no longer enmeshed,

With Satan's sin,
But in what Jesus has begun again.

FORGIVENESS NOMINALIZED

To forgive is worth only a ha'penny,
Merely a sleight of hand for this earth's mortal many.

For lip service is its verbal tender,
In exchange, it has little to offer or render.

Oh, but when forgiveness is more than nominal,
Hearts and souls explode with something phenomenal.

Loss is filled with gain
Due to one holy name.

Hearts once sad,
Are no longer bitter or bad.

It's because of Christ's blood, and its limitless flood,
That human sin is cleansed due to his amends.

His love imbued,
Governs every disposition and mood.

And malevolence that once was,
No longer exists because,

It is spiritual fruit—a sweet red cherry,
Due to God's spiritual apothecary.

FORGIVENESS SANCTIFIED

Set apart, special, unique is what sanctified means.
Holy, untouchable—a concept gloriously keen.

When I think of this word, of being safe from sin,
I'm transported to my youth, playing flag football once again.

Stealing my enemy's flag without being tackled,
Returning victoriously while my team heartily chuckled.

Through forgiveness, God sanctifies us with our own safety zone,
In the promise of heaven, our spiritual home.

In him our souls will never be in jeopardy because of sin,
Because nothing can remove us from his protection.

FORGIVENESS HUMANIZED

One of my cats showed his fellow cat forgiveness,
Instead of succumbing to his natural feline wildness.

It seems a dispute between the two arose over a bowl of food,
His brother stole it from him and thought it not selfish or rude.

He didn't fight, but sat down and then extended his right paw,
Pushing his bowl toward his furry cousin to chew and gnaw.

If it's true that forgiveness is solely a humanized behavior,
How could we have ignored this gift from our Savior?

FORGIVENESS SYNCHRONIZED

Two divers, poised like statues with masculine physiques,
Honed, polished, and sculpted, their god-like forms unique.

Each diver glided effortlessly like wingless eagles through the air,
Until just before the water's surface their bodies prepared.

Synchronizing every muscle and every move,
Slipping through the water's surface, harmlessly and gracefully smooth.

God's forgiveness works in this distinctive fashion,
Its offering perfectly timed, lavish, with boundless compassion.

Therefore, forgiveness should be highly prized,
For its perfection, and how well it's synchronized.

God's mastery is never too early, nor too late,
But at the right moment when we ask for mercy in our sinful state.

Wham! and *Boom!* It's unexpectedly there,
Instant forgiveness for every muscle, sinew, and numbered hair.

FORGIVENESS LEGITIMIZED

The One who was before time and space,
The One smiling on as man attempts a race.

Was he not always there?
Has he not always been everywhere?

Is there not a place he does not know?
Is there nowhere he cannot go?

Oh, foolish man, thou art a laugh,
Before you, he made the neck of a giraffe,

So stop your foolishness of thinking you're smart,
And turn to the one who designed mathematics to create art.

FORGIVENESS IMMORTALIZED

Forgiveness is such a powerful tool,
To give Jesus—not Satan—a chance to rule.
Then why do I choose the latter, making me a fool?

Freely offered, freely given. Perhaps that's the issue.
Something given at no cost isn't valued by an IOU.

But then I thought more deeply about his timely offer,
And I realized it's not free, but came from a red coffer.

Jesus paid the ultimate price with his innocent blood,
His body nailed to a roughly hewn piece of blood-stained wood.

There, on a bald hill, high above Jerusalem town,
He, with two thieves, was made a spectacle by all around.

So no, my forgiveness was not exactly free.
Jesus paid the highest price for me.

FORGIVENESS GLOBALIZED

In times past, few traveled more than a stone's throw away from home,
Ruled more by fear than incentive to roam.

Fiefdoms, city states, and kingdoms, emerged and became out dated,
Replaced by cities, countries, and nations with populations tabulated.

Now the internet connects us, making communication mobile,
But let me tell you about a blessing that's better than global.

God's acceptance knows every tribe, culture, and nation's tongue,
Offering forgiveness to all souls he lives among.

Universal, irreversible, versatile, and adaptable,
Addressing every mortal need no matter how implausible.

He loves to forgive, so to him it isn't a bother.
So, there's no excuse not to reach out to a compassionate Father.

FORGIVENESS HOMOGENIZED

A left-field thought popped into my head
When our cat knocked a glass of milk onto my bread.

Some spilled on the table and then the floor,
To our three cats' culinary glee as they licked up more.

The milk ran in gravity's grip and formed creamy white puddles,
While I used paper towels in quite a panic and anxious muddle.

While watching the milk run in streams of white,
It occurred to me milk and cream blend only in homogenous fights.

Left alone, they tend to separate and go their disparate ways,
But with pasteurizing they are bonded for drinking today.

Left alone, man from God tends to wander and stray,
But then when sin comes calling, he returns, wanting to stay.

Then God forgives, while man fights to be free of his trouble,
And when it's all over, God and man are united again, no longer double.

FORGIVENESS UNAUTHORIZED

Nope! Forgiveness is not for you!
Especially in light of what you do.

He will never see forgiveness's light,
Seems he's always starting a fight.

The trouble she caused by what she said,
Deserves not forgiveness, but retaliation instead.

Where would we be if Jesus thought this way?
Should he have postponed his birth to an undetermined day?

And what say we concerning the brutal cross?

Should he have deferred his death indefinitely,
Until he could see mortals living more piously?

Nope! Forgiveness is not deserved,
It can't be regulated or preserved,
Nor should it be deferred.

THE COLOR OF FORGIVENESS

If you could give forgiveness a color, what would it be?
Would it be as white as the foam on a wave crashing from the sea?

Or perhaps it would be green like pastures dotted with fluffy white sheep,
Then it would cover hill upon hill, from the highest to the valley steep.

If God granted me the honor to choose the color of forgiveness's song,
I would paint it crimson because it covers sins, no matter to whom they
belong.

Red like the sacrificial blood Jesus willingly gave on the unkind cross,
His crimson life flowing where sin counted souls to Satan's gain, but
God's loss.

To Satan's disaster, Jesus defied death, and rose that third day,
Offering eternal forgiveness to all who would in pledge say,

"Glory be to our Father who loves unconditionally,
And through forgiveness, we are eternally free."

Anthology Two

MERCY UNLEASHED

Mercy Unleashed

GOD DIDN'T *OFFER* MERCY. He unleashed it! Let me explain. What comes to mind when something is unleashed?

Trackers unleash dogs chosen for their rare breed as hunters. These canine decedents of the wolf family are uniquely skilled in distinguishing the scent of a fox or raccoon over all other odors. Their owners then give chase in *the hunt*.

Animal rights activists seek pardon for caged lions to run free in open savannahs. Those advocates who are successful have the unparalleled pleasure of observing lions unleashed from the confines of cages or zoos.

Professional equestrian enthusiasts spend small fortunes in boarding, feeding, training, and providing better medical care for their horses than some humans receive. An owner spends his or her energy and countless amounts of money, sometimes for years with only one goal in mind—so the horses can be unleased from a race track's starting gate, run for a mere few minutes, and be the first one over a finish line.

There's a common theme in the visual imagery of these three examples of such exclusive diversity in circumstance. These animals were held at bay until, at man's bidding, they were unleashed, allowing them to run full-throttle—exactly how God delivers mercy to heal the broken soul.

Have you ever pondered that the virtue of mercy has its origin in God? Hence, only he has the ability to grant eternal mercy for a soul's salvation. Man can practice mercy on earth, along with forgiveness and grace. However, man's mercy is time-based because it is extended by a mortal, and ultimately ends in the grave. God's mercy, though, was released at the cross. As Christ's blood flowed, mercy leapt from the cross in a tsunami of love spreading salvation throughout the world.

This is why I believe God's mercy is not so much offered or given, but unleashed. God is excited about showering us in his mercy. That is why Jesus died so that God's mercy could be unleashed.

Christ's death broke the dogs' leashes, opened the lions' cages, and set the race horses free to run as fast as their hearts could pump blood into their muscles.

MERCY'S JOY

Oh, what joy mercy brings.
It causes angles in heaven to sing.

Oh, how mercy fully covers
Our hearts, forgiving sin as it hovers.

What joy does mercy ignite
As it ushers in heaven's twilight?

Pray thee, tell me, kind sir or ma'am,
Can any other virtue remove my damn?

No! Only in Jesus do we possess,
What only he on a tree did finesse.

By his blood he removed Satan's stress,
And gave to his followers new holiness.

MERCY AS GOD'S ARTISTRY

Who inspired Michael Angelo?
What artistic womb birthed Picasso?

Was it just a matter of genetic DNA?

No, their canvases were alive
because in God's mind they reached to thrive.

It was God himself who divinely spoke,
Bringing life with every careful brush stroke.

Mercy is the artwork of God,
Superficially this statement may seem odd,

But closely examine a sin-damaged soul,
See mercy paint a crimson picture destroying sin's toll.

Each caring stroke of the brush of God's love,
Brings his children closer to his home above.

Then upon the finished canvas of salvation,
Emerges an image of life in his kingdom nation.

MERCY REMOVES DEATH'S STING

Woe betide death,
God lead me to the moment of my life's last breath.

Does death really sting?
What consequences does death bring?

What, after life, is next?
Do not leave me unprepared and vexed.

My child, live without doubt.
Mercy makes death's victim shout.

For at mortal's last exhale,
Two closed eyes will see four bloodied, iron nails,

Which in their dastardly devilish work,
Delivered sinners from Satan's angry smirk.

And all believers have one chore,
To accept a pardon, nothing more.

MERCY CHALLENGED

Mercy is challenged every day,
Satan looks for our weaknesses in every way.

I shouldn't have said or done this or that,
Now I've failed my Lord of pardon completely flat.

It's in this critical moment we temporarily lose sight,
That it's not us, but Jesus's blood that Satan fights.

So don't fall for this trick from our wicked antediluvian foe,
And always remember—your name, our Father personally knows.

For once we've been washed clean of every stain,
We remain pure and holy in his gracious name.

MERCY'S FACE

Did you know mercy has a face?
It can be found in every nation's race,
So powerful, it changes life's grueling pace.

"What does it resemble?" you ask.
It's so pleasantly brazen it should be on bottle and flask,
Once experienced, it changes life's every task.

There are eyes inviting sinners all,
As lips gently whisper a pardon's call,
And ears understand each other's fall.

Was this not the face of Christ Jesus?
Did he not come to offer forgiveness?
Therefore, let us wear his face in thankfulness.

MERCY SETTLES THE SCORE

What say you about this war?
Are God and Satan only settling a score?
Being caught in their crossfire is such a bore.

Oh, but this is not the case,
For you see we're all in a race.

Time is short and at its end we'll give report.

No, this is not a war between Satan and Savior,
But between ourselves and our wanton behavior.

Satan can't make us do anything we're against,
Our concession to sin causes offense.

This is why mercy is so vital,
Through it we receive a royal title.

Christ's red river flows with redemption's purchase,
Satan and his angels can no longer besmirch us.

MERCY'S ADVICE

If asked, what pearl of wisdom would be mercy's advice?
A rare philosophical pondering perhaps, thought once or thrice,

But truly, what would she suggest is her forte?
Does she indeed have a plum-line by which to walk each day?

I believe she would purport and suggest,
That where a mortal heart beats in a human chest,
Lives a soul in God's house that is always welcome and blessed.

MERCY NEVER LOST

Could there be a sin in which
We find our souls wallowing in an immoral ditch,
Because we swallowed Satan's tempting pitch?

Though we mortals sometimes feel it so,
And allow guilt's weight to bring us low,
We've misunderstood mercy's bright glow.

Mercy is all about
Making us stand up and shout
"I'm forgiven and there's no doubt!"

Sin can no longer cast its dark shadow
To frighten my soul and make it bellow,
Because Christ's blood makes me hallow.

MERCY'S PAUSE

Does mercy sometimes take a pause?
Should it reconsider a specific moral cause?

Could it have a time of hesitancy
When it debates a soul's worth for eternity,
When considering spiritual candidacy?

Does it pick and choose only the best?
Do only the deserving pass its test?

Satan would have us to believe this way,
Because our guilt gives him another day.

But a resounding *No* is mercy's answer,
As it seeks to deliver all from sin's cancer.

Because we serve a God, who has just one order,
Mercy is offered to all in every quarter.

MERCY'S RECOIL

Mercy recoils like blazing cannons on the line.
It explodes with power, but equally, returns in time.

The blast is so overwhelming and utterly complete,
That Satan, in rebuttal, can't compete.

It sears with a royal crimson stain,
No sin can cling; no sin remains.

What Jesus accomplished with mercy, through his blood,
Brings a second message to be understood.

Mercy, not only given, but generously received,
Offers full pardon to all whom in him believed.

MERCY SOUGHT

Mercy sought is an impossibility,
Because it was bought for you and me.

It's free to whomever asks.
To acquire? Only one simple task.

Lay down,
Face to the ground,

Then in simple humility,
Embrace his pardon openly.

Your sin his love will warmly cover,
And you can start a new life over.

SAVE YOUR LAST DANCE FOR MERCY

Dancing is a beautiful art
For the old in flesh and young at heart.

Dancers swing and twirl,
Always ready to give another whirl.

But before each partner looms a universal fate,
A last dance before standing at the pearly gate.

Our last dance in life will bring a setting sun.
There is no escape from death's final run.

Have we accepted mercy as our eternal partner?
No matter who else we try, none other will garner,

A waltz, a gala replete with musical tunes,
A partner of pardon to lift us beyond other planets and moons.

MERCY'S WAIT

Why does mercy wait at a lost heart's dark door?
Why does it patiently knock evermore?

Forgiveness has more than what we thought it had in store.

Mercy waits with the strength of humility and grace.
Mercy waits because it's seen the Father's perfect, holy face.

But Mercy's greatest gift is not in its gentle, persistent presence.
Mercy's benefit is the crimson stain, and forgiveness is its essence.

MERCY'S CONCEPTION

Long before there was time,
When all existence was sublime,
Not even Satan could say, "This soul is mine."

God conceived mercy.

When angels came and went,
Because their Lord on missions sent,
And they returned to him sound with intent.

God conceived mercy.

When there was no concept of space,
Nor possession, or the idea of place,
Because great and small lived interlaced.

God conceived mercy.

Breathing was not necessary,
And there was no need for apothecary,
As illness could not be found in heaven's dictionary.

God conceived mercy.

Why, you may ask
Did God self-assign this task?

Because God foreknew and wept
Over man, and in his heart he kept
A path to redemption,
A covering for transgression,

When man chose sin, embracing Satan's bet.

God so loved man, he conceived mercy.

Anthology Three

HASTEN TO GRACE

Hasten to God's Grace

WE SEE IT ALL the time in movies. After a desperate struggle between the hero and villain at the climax of a story plot, the villain falls over a cliff edge where he fearfully hangs dangling by one hand, between life and death.

The hero doesn't have to do anything except wait for the villain to lose his grip when his aching hand muscles tire and he can't hold his body weight any longer. Then he will tumble to his death into the vast jungle abyss, hundreds of feet below. Hungry crocodiles raise their grotesque heads exposing their razor-sharp teeth anxiously waiting to dine on his flesh.

At this juncture of the plot, the hero faces his toughest decision so far in the story line. Does he extend grace by rescuing the villain, or does he let the rogue reap the grim reward of his evil deeds? No one can fault the hero if he lets the villain meet his maker. In fact, probably most of the audience is rooting for the hero to release the scoundrel's hand. The villain's demise is justified because he and no one else made the delinquent choices that killed or harmed other characters in the action adventure.

But, as the camera zooms in on the hero's face, the audience can see a change in his eyes, then slowly his facial expression exhibits forgiveness. Suddenly, what he's wanted to do throughout the story, he cannot. He has talked about it, imagined it, and sworn an oath to accomplish it. However, now that he's finally arrived at a time when he can fulfill his dark ambition, the hero discovers he is unable to follow through.

Hence, the hero inches up to the cusp of the ledge, extends his hand, and pulls the villain to safety. The bad guy can't believe what just happened. If the roles were reversed, he would have let the hero fall to his death. So why did the hero save him?

The answer to the villain's question is found in one word. Grace. In ancient Greek, grace is defined as unmerited favor. In movie jargon this definition means the hero offers a hand of salvation. You see, grace is not about deserving clemency. Grace is about uprooting and turning justice on its head.

Grace means a rescue from what justice demands.
Jesus is our hero. That's why we need to grasp his hand.

GRACE IS GOD'S GIFT

What is it about the human race?
Because we cannot see God's face,

We think He doesn't exist and rule.
I think it's man who is the fool.

God exists in every smile,
His glory lingers for more than a while.

His beauty reflected in his daughter, Eve,
And in his son, Adam whom he first conceived.

Though his realm is beyond man's imagination,
He lives in each heart of his creation.

Therefore, let's not question his eternal existence,
Because he provides for us more than earthly subsistence.

One day we will gaze upon his glorious presence,
And live with him in grace, just one of his many presents.

GRACE FREES US FROM WORRY

Worry!
A single solitary flurry,
A unique ingredient in a recipe, leaving us surly.

Wonder if Jesus felt it in some way?
Did it consume him like it does us for more than a day?
Or did he give it to his father, anticipating what he would say?
Then filled with the Spirit what attitude did he display?

Hear his prayer on the Mount of Olives when he was alone,
When man and Satan sought the marrow from his bone,
Though he prayed, "Remove this cup!" We've been shown
He accepted God's will, our sin to atone.

And in this grace given from the Father to Son,
Jesus showed us how not to worry from sun to sun.

GRACE OFFERS A PATH BEYOND THE CLOUDS

How high can I fly?
Not with birds or clouds in the sky,

But how far will my soul reach?
Is there a boundary to breach?

Soaring straight to heaven is where I wish to go,
Confident my God will grant me to know

The untold limits of his mercy and grace.
Oh, to grant me, a sinner, to one day see his face.

Lord, I thank you for your unconditional pardon,
At death my soul will live in a perfect new garden.

GOD'S GRACE IS INESCAPABLE

Why do I think I can hide my humbling disgrace?
No place on earth nor in heaven hides from your face!

Is there a rock, or mountain, or forest, or any concealing place?
Is there anywhere we aren't covered by your forgiving grace?

Could there be another who would accept me, a mortal so base?
Who else but you in compassion's rapture aches to embrace?

When all others forsake me, you seek my soul in a holy chase.
Therefore, I surrender my heart to you as one healed and no longer
debased.

GRACE'S TIME IS NOW

The time is now
For all to bow
Before the King of what and how.

For there's no other
We claim as Brother
Through whom our sins become washed over.

Only he gave his blood,
Only he before Satan stood,
Only he rightly could.

THE GRACE DEBATE

The grace debate—
Some feel mercy can be too late.
Others feel forgiveness has no certain date
For Christians who are in a poor spiritual state.

Is it not God who decides?
Is he not always by his believers' sides?
In the bordello, parlors of shame woe betide,
He seeks souls, regardless.

Jealousy, greed, envy, and pride,
There's no sin his creation can hide.

Only he knows exactly what's in each heart,
Only he can discern instantly when his children depart.
Therefore, let all recognize he alone possesses the saving art,
To prepare souls to begin an eternal new start.

GRACE IS FRUSTRATING

Sometimes I must admit,
Understanding God gives me a fit.

I know he's God and I am man,
But he seems so unfair after I've done all I can.

I say my prayers twice a day,
I watch what I think, do, and say.

But nothing works out as I thought it would.
I wonder, has he done all he could?

But when I have doubted him the most,
I am moved by his Holy Ghost.

He reminds me his grace is as good as it gets,
Because his son died so I'd have no regrets.

GRACE IS AN INVITATION TO THE LORD'S TABLE

If not for the Lord's grace,
The world would know my disgrace.

In reverence I bow down, hiding my face.

He then touches my shoulder, bidding me rise up
To look to his Son tasting the bitter cup.

He then invites me to his table to sup.

WHO BUT GOD CAN OFFER GRACE?

Oh, what shallow false steps we take
When first we choose not to surrender but negotiate,
So that we will one day enter the holy gate.

But then, somewhere along life's hazardous way,
We lose our resolution to permanently stay,
And then we can't navigate one single day.

Stumble, trip, and fall we do,
As life twirls in circles as in a cauldron of boiling stew,
And our lives once seemingly peaceful become difficult to do.

It's at this jarring juncture,
That the perfect life we thought we had receives a puncture.
But it's not too late to fully surrender and receive God's promised picture.

GRACE PARDONS MY TONGUE

"My Lord did I dare?"
I heard my unbridled tongue swear.

Why did these foul words pass over my lips?
How low did I in darkness spontaneously dip?

My tongue promises never to do it again,
Then I feel the first couple's sin crawling under my skin.

What boils my blood to this precipice in my being?
Why to this vow I find so difficult to cling?

It's his blood that removes my sins' dross.
Thanks be to Jesus who died on the cross,
That in these moments there's no personal loss.

GRACE IS A PASSAGE INTO THE ETERNAL

Oh, permanent rest,
At the end will I have done my best?

Oh, perpetual slumber,
When Jesus returns will I be in his number?

Oh, perpetuities of heaven's holy gift,
At the end will he my soul from this life lift?

My guarantee is not in labor's perspiration on my face.
It's singularly gifted in Jesus's saving grace.

IS THERE A PLACE FOR ME IN GOD'S GRACE?

When I see my life as a total disgrace,
Pray tell how can I dare to seek his face?

Then I think of a tax collector in a tree he pardoned,
And an adulterous woman he forgave and didn't bargain.

Was there not a woman at a well whose heart he softened?
And a thief on a cross into paradise he welcomed?
Oh Lord, your grace gives me hope emboldened.

So, I bow down to the One and Only
Who is willing to forgive this one so lonely.
Because by his Son's blood I can approach his throne boldly
And be given a heavenly home so comely.

MAN'S RIGHTS ARE FOUND IN GRACE

Man demands he has rights!
Pushing him to engage in numerous fights.
History records him defending them with all his might.

Are his rights universal?
Definitions are varied, and controversial.

So perhaps to determine what they are,
Turn away from man, and look beyond the Morning Star.

For there are no rights of man, except one,
And that's to fear God and serve him until his time is done.

THROUGH GRACE I'LL SEE GOD'S FACE

Lord, I wrestle every day,
With what I keep inside, safe from display.

How can I make room for you
When I'm filled with what I say and do?

This demon of my flesh and bone,
Draws me away from my heavenly home.

How I long for the day I'll gaze upon your face.
Thank you, Lord, for your unending grace.

GRACE HAS NO MEMORY

In grace, there's no memory
Of sin's seeming impunity.

Only of freedom's liberty,
And our souls' holy recovery.

All because of a discovery,
A cleansing from impurity,
By the blood of Triune royalty.

GOD'S GRACE IS MY LIFE-SOURCE

God's grace pumps blood through my heart.
God's grace gives the beauty of love and art.

God's grace fills my lungs with each breath of air.
God's grace puts me in his dependable care.

God's grace is in each beat of my pulse.
God's Grace answers my prayers with results.

God, please forgive me when I try to live without you.
Discipline me when you see what I do.

Gently return me to your fold, despite my spiritual blindness
Like the loving Father of mercy and kindness.

THE MIRACLE OF GRACE ON THE APPOINTED DAY

In my weakness, you are glorified,
In my frailty, you are magnified.
Saved from sin, I am sanctified.

Though I was once lost,
Your blood paid the cost.

Praise him, who is merciful and full of grace,
For on that appointed day, we'll bow before his perfect face.

GRACE ABOUNDS

Oh, grace where do you abound?
Where least expected are you found?

Was it not the thief who died on the cross
Who felt both this and the next life a loss?

Yet, in the time it takes to blink an eye,
Jesus told him after this earth, he would never die.

Where is found such healing compassion?
Where is found this undying passion?

It can only come from the God of mercy,
Who at death, raises souls from earth and sea.

AWED BY A PERFECT GOD

I'm awed
By a perfect God.
From where does he possess his mercy?
What is the source of his divine courtesy?

I'm awed
By a perfect God.
To what does he ascribe absolute forgiveness?
Why waste his precious time in the saving business?

I'm awed
By a perfect God,
Because he cares about me,
Even though I'm drowning in Satan's sea.

Then, just when Satan is about to pull me under,
I hear from heaven a mighty clap of thunder,
And God's hand reaches down from his throne,
To carry me up to his heavenly home.

GRACE FOR YOU AND ME

Grace unto you and me,
The reason for which I cannot see.

Dare I ponder why?
Does God not my sins decry?

Yet grace purchased cannot resist
Embracing us, hand over fist.

No matter how guilt does dispel,
God knows us, oh, so well.

He offers what can only be given,
As he wants us with him in his heaven.

HEAVEN'S GATE

Heaven's gate.
Does it await my fate?
Is it a myth we perpetuate?

To arrive at heaven's portal,
Is not a fate for every mortal,
Though this has been believed for time immemorial.

Eternal destiny is of God's Grace,
Given freely to each repenting face,
Granting broken souls a permanent, holy place.

GOD IS GRACIOUS

God is gracious, God is good.
And for this blessing we know what we should.
But we have in darkness done what we could,
Knowing all too well what he desires we would.

God is gracious, God is forgiving.
He alone forgives the living.
Since his son did all the giving,
We will live as an eternal being.

GRACE'S GIFTS ARE CERTAIN

Grace has given
Forgiveness for sins hidden.

It pardons unconditionally,
Restores mercifully.

We deserve not what it offers.
It consoles what our consciences suffer,

Then leads to a new way,
To live with Jesus every day.

CHOSEN BY GRACE

Chosen by grace,
No need to conceal my face.
Redeemed by grace,
No longer in shame's disgrace.

Retribution won't be part of my eternity,
Because salvation's cost is not paid by any treasury.

Praise God for his eternal plan,
Offered to every woman and man.

HOW I KNOW GRACE WORKS

How do I know grace works?
The way it's designed seems to have quirks.

It doesn't really make any sense.
All I need is repentance?

What about justice and law?
Seems going unpunished has an inherent flaw.

Oh, but you see, once came a voice,
"Grace for sin could have no other choice.

Two thousand years ago justice was served,
When an innocent man died for what he didn't deserve.

Through his death all are free,
Grace paid the price for you and me."

REACH FOR GRACE

Go ahead and reach for it!
Don't let doubt hinder a longing spirit.

There it is within your grasp!
Let not hesitancy sting like the viper or asp.

Can you taste it? It's just right there.
Self-mistrust can't impede the hunger's stare.

Better a quest to give your all,
Than a cynical glare from standing tall.

For achievement beyond self isn't found in you or me.
Return to a garden and learn of sin's certain tree.

Stop forging ahead boldly on your own to do or die,
Instead, cast your reach toward heaven's beckoning sky.

WHEN I CLOSE MY EYES

I close my eyes and see his face,
You know the One, of saving grace.
His mercy given for my shame's disgrace,
Though tough, it's as delicate as lace.

His grace is marked by blood and pain,
Not to be confused with something inane.
It reaches from a tomb which is Satan's bane,
And at Christ's return will be his disdain.

Praise God for his grace which easily covers,
Because he gives us his Spirit which around us hovers.
No matter what we've done, we'll readily discover
Salvation through grace given by no other.

Conclusion

I HAVE BEEN A counselor for nearly forty years. In my work I encountered a multitude of broken marriages and shattered families. With each splintered relationship, I employed traditional therapeutic techniques. However, no man-made system I learned in graduate school ever healed these fractured lives as successfully as the three virtues that are the subject of this book.

Forgiveness, mercy, and grace can melt ice-cold, frozen hearts. These virtues are like the surgeon's needle and thread sewing together two pieces of torn flesh. These gifts cross the no-man's land full of barbed wire, land-mines, mud, machine guns, mortars, and cannons for one purpose only—to wave the white flag of surrender so that negotiations between the enemies will lead to peace.

You may say, "I just can't forgive! Too much has happened."

"There's no way I'll show mercy!"

"No mercy has been shown to me."

And finally, "Grace? How can I offer grace? You don't know what he did to me."

Now let the words Jesus uttered while he hung on the Cross echo through your heart and soul. "Father forgive them for they do not know what they are doing." (Luke 23:34) NIV

Two concepts I hope you gained from reading these poems: First, no matter what you have said or done, Jesus has forgiven you and washed you in his mercy by offering you grace. Second, if he can offer forgiveness, mercy, and grace to heal our souls, then we can do the same in our relationships.

> "A righteous man may have many troubles, but the Lord delivers him from them all; he protects all his bones, not one of them will be broken." (Psalm 34:19–20) NIV